THE ROAD TO HAPPINESS

How To Get What You *Really* Want

DAVID GOLDMAN

INDIE BOOKS
INTERNATIONAL

ISBN-10: 1-947480-80-4
ISBN-13: 978-1-947480-80-3
Library of Congress Control Number: 2019916611

Designed by Joni McPherson, mcphersongraphics.com

INDIE BOOKS INTERNATIONAL, INC.
2424 VISTA WAY, SUITE 316
OCEANSIDE, CA 92054
www.indiebooksintl.com

PRAISE FOR THE ROAD TO HAPPINESS

"The biggest benefit to working with David has come from his ability to customize a program that fits my current need. In over a decade of working with David my needs have changed and so has his ability to help me. All the prior training I've had in a very long career was meant to have me change to fit the training. David listens to my desired objective and customizes a program to help me get there. The next best thing to working with David Goldman personally is reading his book."

Mike Kauffelt, Former President and CEO at Bill Few Associates

"I wish David showed up in my life sooner. I was in a family business and partnership with my older brother for seventeen years. We had a lot of philosophical differences in the last two of those years. David helped me transition through these most difficult of times. Eighteen years later I have

a new business partner with sales at six times what I was previously making. The greatest thing about working with David is that my family and life are whole again. David helped me to be the best version of a husband, father, son, brother and business owner that I could ever imagine. I've been waiting years for this awesome information to be put in book form. I'm a true disciple of the Goldman philosophies. I traveled the Road to Happiness with David's help, and guess what? I really got what I wanted."

Larry Albensi, President of Maverick Dental Labs Inc.

"Begin with a title that resonates with what all humans are trying to find in life — Happiness! In his writings, David Goldman shares years of hands-on, real, experience that has helped so many find their way (including many I have referred over the years). Never one to disappoint, in his book David shares his coaching principles and approach to individual success, while also sharing related stories that let you know, it is not a straight line. Keep this book at your bedside, so that you can start with

*the vision of your ideal day, leading to building an
ideal life of happiness."*

**Ann Dugan, Founder of Institute for Entrepreneurial
Excellence at University of Pittsburgh, Senior
Managing Director, Advisory & Education Services**

*"I know that David Goldman can speak and sing,
but that he can write is extraordinarily good news,
especially for those of us searching for a path to
happiness. The beauty of David's prescription is in
its simplicity: live life by design. Find your strength.
Do what matters. Be kind to yourself. One can
hear David's voice in each sentence. His writing
is genuine and resonates. He generously shares
his wisdom, and his passion for helping others is
palpable. Though I have learned much from David
over the years, I found new insights in the pages of
The Road to Happiness. As David suggests, life is
a contest where the winners read the most books.
Place this one on your short list. Oh, and David, I
never told you, but I graduated from Harvard."*

Steven D. Irwin, Partner at LEECH/TISHMAN Law Firm

"I met David Goldman in 2002 shortly after I lost my job in the broadcasting industry. Over the years, David has talked about writing a book about how people create their own roadblocks to success, The Road To Happiness was worth the wait. There are many self-help books in the market and more are published every day. The difference with David is the real stories about real people with real problems. As he told me when we first met, he 'helps people get to the next level in their lives.' The stories reveal how people can change once someone takes the time to listen, understand, and help them understand themselves. The Road To Happiness should be required reading for anyone whose self-doubts create barriers to achieving goals. I thoroughly enjoyed reading it and I learned some things about myself."

Dick Singer, Master Chair, Vistage International

"David has written the quintessential book for people who want to be outstanding in their chosen field. In your hands you hold a treasure chest of wisdom, insight, principles, and ideas that can take

*you from where you are today to a place you have
always wanted to go. Read carefully, apply liberally
and exceed your expectations! You will be glad you
did and will never be the same."*

**Mark LeBlanc, CSP, author of *Growing Your
Business* and *Defining YOU***

*"This book is a masterful weaving of real-life stories
to address what we all can relate to in one way or
another. It is an opportunity to find ourselves in the
examples of others. It is an easy read with amazing
insights that get to the point and allow us to look
at areas where we can bring more happiness into
our lives, both personally and professionally. David
is one of those people who asks the right questions
at the right time. Each chapter gives us a chance to
ponder the deeper wisdom within us and that really
is where the secret to happiness lives, when we
get to that place, what we really want manifests in
amazing ways. The evidence of that is in the stories
here. I love this book!"*

**Kathy Larsen, Clarity Coach and Intuition Guide,
HeartLight Connection, LLC**

"Don't be fooled by the length of this breezy little gem of a book. It's loaded with wisdom and dozens of tips for taking action on whatever you want to change or improve, whether it's your whole life or just a slice of it."

Chris Posti, Author, The Shortest Distance Between You And Your New Job, Career and Executive Coach and Columnist

"Success without happiness is very unfulfilling. In The Road To Happiness, David Goldman shares real stories and practical tips on how to choose to become happier, which leads to a more fulfilling and successful life. I especially liked the Appendix, where David shares his proven Goldman Enrollment Process and his G.O.L.D. Attitudes. I highly recommend this book for you and others who want to get on the road to happiness."

Patrick Donadio, CSP, MCC, Speaker, Executive Coach, and author of Communicating with IMPACT

"For years, I've watched and listened as David shared inspirational stories and pearls of life and business wisdom, exclaiming at every turn: 'You

*should write a book!' Well, he has, and it was
worth the wait. This book is filled with great life
lessons about the power of motivation — and the
successes that come from its application."*
**Paul Furiga, President and Chief Storyteller,
WordWrite Communications, Inc**

*"I jokingly refer to my discussions with David
as my moments with King Solomon who was
considered the wisest man on earth. David has a
wealth of knowledge about business and life that
is always relevant. David's passion for reading and
re-reading the best business books, like 7 Habits
of Highly Effective People, have made him an
invaluable friend and mentor. What I like most is
that he can recite passages of these books that
apply to everyday issues in a way that nails the
solution eloquently and persuasively. Anyone who is
fortunate enough to employ David as their business
coach can count on incredible results by following
his prescriptions."*
Jim Owens, President, CallPRO, Inc

"I have been an attorney for nineteen years now. Of those nineteen years, twelve have been as president of Michael W. Nalli, P.C, a law firm of which I am the sole shareholder. I have called upon David Goldman at two very crucial times in this twelve-year period: first, during the planning phases of my law firm, and second, during what I will call my bout with mid-life crisis in which I was planning an exodus from my law firm and from the law practice in general. Without David's guidance, wisdom, listening skills, and most importantly his candor, I would not be in the position that I am in now in my career: that of enjoying what I do and earning more than I ever have. I equate David's coaching acumen to that of the great coaches in the sporting world over the years. He challenges you to be better by focusing on details that are right in front of you, but choose to ignore. He challenges you to creatively market to your clients the value proposition for your services, and in the process abandon the old business models and methods of thinking. In short, without David's guidance over the past twelve years, I would not have the quality of life that I have in

balancing work and family. My only regret is not listening to David's advice sooner."

Michael W. Nalli, Esq., President, Michael W. Nalli, P.C.

"I've worked closely with and recommended David to my friends, colleagues, and clients countless times over the last twenty-five years. His results continue to impress. In his book, The Road To Happiness, David demonstrates his incredible skills and the wealth of knowledge that he's accumulated to help his clients get what they truly want. If you're looking achieve what you truly want, this book is a must-read."

**John H. Iannucci, J.D., LLM, The Iannucci
Law Group, P.C.**

CONTENTS

INTRODUCTION

When John Lennon, of the Beatles, was in the fourth grade, his teacher gave the class an assignment, which was only one question. "What do you want to be when you grow up?" The class gave a variety of responses. When she came to John, he said, "I want to be happy." The teacher responded, "You don't understand the assignment." Lennon replied, "You don't understand *life.*"

Do you?

If you ask Japanese women to describe in one word what they want for their children, they will say *success*. If you ask the same question of American women, they will answer *happiness*.

People are searching for happiness, but what is that? Is it success? Achievement? Hitting your goals? Is it a feeling? What do you think?

In the early 1990s, I heard Jack Canfield speak about a California study that asked people from all walks of life, of both genders, age twenty-two to seventy-two, one question: "What do you wish you had learned in school, but they didn't teach it?" Good question. How about you? What do you wish you had learned?

There were six top answers to the survey:

1. How to accept (like) myself

2. How to get along with others

3. How to set goals

4. How to organize myself

5. How to make money and keep it

6. How to communicate better

In 1989, when I started my business, I decided to teach, consult, and coach people on how to communicate more effectively so that they could make more money. I focused on business owners and salespeople.

Five or six years earlier, in 1983–84, I'd had the opportunity to study with Fernando Flores, who taught that when we communicate, we speak and hear through filters. This revelation, along with Stephen Covey's habit number five (of the *7 Habits of Highly Effective People* — seek first to understand before being understood), became the basis of my coaching program.[1]

I even wrote a chapter in the book *The Sales Coach* (published in 1997) titled, "Are You Listening?" It described both Covey's and Flores's concepts in detail. I thought that communication, and listening in particular, was the key to enhanced results.[2]

---

[1] Stephen R. Covey, *The 7 Habits of Highly Effective People* (Provo, UT: Franklin Covey, 1998).

[2] David Goldman, "Are You Listening?," chapter, in *The Sales Coach: Selling Tips from the Pros* (Monroeville, PA.: Jeffrey Tobe, 1997)

Here's what Flores taught: when you control your own filter and take into consideration (and respect) the other person's filter, you have a chance at true communication. This applies to your relationships at work, in life, and with yourself.

The 7 Habits of Highly Effective People was the first model that I used, adding Flores's work in the communication section. It worked very well for the first few years. When I heard about the California study, the whole process made more sense and was easier to explain to potential clients. The first four topics in the survey formed the foundation that supports communication for results.

The past thirty years have been a wild ride. The results for my clients have been outstanding, and as a result, I have carved out a life and a lifestyle business that I love.

An interesting thing happened along the way. With the help of my coach, Mark LeBlanc, I discovered a fascinating concept, and thus the basis of this book.

It's not a new concept, and it's probably one you have heard before. You teach that which you most need to learn. It was no different for me. Over the past thirty years, I needed to listen better. As they say in the play *Hamilton*, "Talk less; smile more!" As I became a better listener, my business grew, and so did I. I became a better coach and a better human being. If that were the end of the story, it would be a good one.

However, another path also became very clear to me — one where the journey has been longer, more arduous, and more common among human beings. Yes, we can all learn to be better listeners, better communicators, and better service providers. The other path deals with something even more valuable, more essential to finding happiness.

Many people fall into the trap of thinking that (fill in the blank) will make you happy — more money, new house, new car, new clothes, more love, more time, more balance, etc.

Those are all nice things, but that ain't it! It's much deeper than all of those things.

What follows are stories that illustrate an interesting phenomenon. The stories are true. The names have been changed to protect the client and preserve confidentiality agreements. In each case, the person hired me in order to get a desired result. It was what they perceived that they wanted most. However, along the way, each one found something they wanted that was even *more* valuable. They found the key that unlocks the vault which contains their ultimate desire.

Why is that important? My mission is to have people get what they *really* want and be happy. Because happy people do not hurt other people. When you are happy with yourself, you have no need to hurt someone else. Your world and *the* world is a better place.

As you begin the journey of reading this book, I hope that you, too, will find a key that helps to unlock your vault. Furthermore, I hope you enjoy the journey.

1

YOUR KIDS DON'T EVEN KNOW WHO YOU ARE

B y most accounts, you would say Joe was very successful. He had been a financial advisor for well over fifteen years and had a thriving practice. He was making good money, had a great house in the suburbs, a wife, two kids, and a couple of cars. All in all, he was living The American Dream.

When we had our initial interview, Joe told me that there were two main issues he wanted help with: time management and behavioral adjustment. Joe is a fun-loving guy who, frankly, sometimes goes too far and gets himself into trouble. Nothing too serious, but he had been written up at work a few times and had been told to modify his behavior on many occasions.

Equally as important, Joe spent a lot of time at the office and rarely saw his kids. In fact, his wife remarked that his daughter (ninth grade) and son (sixth grade), were going to be out of the house in a few years and they didn't even know him very well.

So, Joe was hiring me for two reasons: (1) He wanted to change or at least modify his behavior, and (2) Without reducing his income, he wanted to spend more time with his children and establish a good relationship with them before they were gone and on their own.

As often happens, the journey we began became much more impactful than we thought it would. What started as behavior modification became a quest for self-acceptance. For various reasons, Joe was not happy with who he was and therefore acted out when confronted with feelings of inadequacy. Joe had come from a blue-collar background and never went to college. This turned out to be a very big deal. Joe was ashamed of himself and never felt comfortable dealing with other professionals.

Quite simply, he felt *less than* and unworthy. So, he would do things in excess.

We embarked on a journey toward Joe liking himself for who he was and actually being okay with being Joe.

Within weeks, Joe was making better choices and behaving in a way that was consistent with who he wanted to be as a man. He envisioned the person he wanted to be, and slowly but surely, he became that guy.

> I'm not saying that going to college isn't important. I think it's a great opportunity for most people. You can learn a trade or profession that leads to future work. More

> importantly, you can receive an education
> that prepares you for living life in a certain
> way. Most importantly, it provides an early
> example of completion for a young person. It's
> something you can say you accomplished.

Joe realized that he could never go back and experience college as a teenager/young adult. He also realized that having a degree might be important if you are currently looking for a job. However, he finally came to realize that being a successful financial advisor for many years was worth something.

In fact, it was worth *a lot more*. He had actually built something from scratch, on his own, and was thriving. He was, after all, successful *in spite of* not having attended or graduated college. Maybe even *because* he never went to college.

No matter how he had felt in the past about what he had or hadn't accomplished, he could feel good about what he had achieved in his business and in his life. More importantly, he could now begin to appreciate who he was and what he does for his clients and for his family. *Joe is a good man.*

The time management issue was a different challenge. First, we adjusted Joe's mindset that to be a successful financial advisor, one must put in a lot of hours: Leave home early to get to the office, stay all day, get home late. You know the drill. It's a work ethic that was born in the United States Rust Belt, of a labor-intensive heritage that says you have to work long and hard to survive.

I'm not suggesting that hard work isn't important. Neither am I saying "Work smart; not hard." I hate that cliché. Hard work is important, and there is no substitute for it.

It's how you define it, however, that really counts. Work hard on the things that count the most toward your ultimate goal. Determine your highest-value activities and work hard at doing those. That's what Joe and I worked to achieve with his day.

One part of my coaching program that has
an impact on most people is the concept of
an Ideal Day and an Ideal Week. When I first
learned this in the late 1980s, it changed my
life, and it has improved many others' lives
as well. There are twenty-four hours in a day
and seven days in a week. That's not news.
It's the arithmetic that is powerful. 24 × 7 =
168. There are 168 hours in each week. How
you use them determines the quality of your
life. Decide what time you will wake up in
the morning and then determine the best use
of every hour you are awake during the day.
That will depend on your goals and priorities.
Include everything that is important to you.
This is the key to designing the life you want
to live. You must structure it — day by day,
hour by hour, step by step.

Joe finally understood the notion that it's not the
hours you put in that count; it's what you *put into
the hours*. With my guidance, he designed and

constructed what an ideal day and an ideal week would look like. This included spending afternoons, some evenings, and weekends with his family, and especially his kids. We established (with their input) what one-on-one time with each would entail.

All that was left was to implement the plan. I'm proud and happy to report that within one year, Joe had not only established relationships with his children but improved overall relationships with his family as a whole.

In addition, he became more efficient and more effective with his hours at work and doubled his income in the process. Needless to say, Joe and his family were ecstatic about the results he produced. He was making twice the revenue in half the time.

Today, fifteen years later, Joe is still happily married, both children are married with children of their own, and Joe is a proud father and grandfather and husband loved by family, friends, clients, and associates. His income has doubled again, and he's earning in excess of five times where he was when I met him.

So, how about you? What thinking is holding you back from being happy with yourself and achieving what you really want? Where are you spending (wasting) time that could be put to greater use? Design your ideal week and live into the dream.

2

THERE IS NO SUCH THING AS *BALANCE*

I met Sherry at a speed networking event. She was extremely attractive and appeared very self-assured. Blonde, blue-eyed, and statuesque, she commanded most rooms she walked into. A sales rep for an advertising firm, she seemed to have it all.

Like speed dating, speed networking is a timed event at which each person has a minute or two to engage with the person across from them to see if there's a connection or fit. As I described, Sherry is stunning, and I mentioned to her that how she looked spoke so loudly, I could barely hear what she had to say.

She specialized in creating branding and ad campaigns for major companies. I mentioned that I worked with salespeople who wanted to make more money and enjoy their life. She said, "I'm looking for more balance in my life." I said, "There is no such thing as balance...only priorities. You want to do what you want to do when you want to do it."

She said, "No one has ever explained it like that to me before. Let's have coffee sometime!"

I said, "OK," and took out my calendar.

Experience has taught me to strike while the iron is hot. It might appear cool to just suggest "my people get in touch with your people" to set up a meeting, but phone tag and email tag aren't games that are fun to play. So, make sure you don't look desperate or needy.

Change your mindset. Come from a place
of, "Let's get this on the calendar" while the
mood is right and interest is high.

Sherry hired me to increase sales, make more money,
and have a better all-around life with her family
(husband and two kids). She was also interested in
being clear about her purpose and overall goals in life.

Like most salespeople I work with, Sherry was
already masterful and produced very strong results.
This was not about learning how to close sales
or making sure she focused on the customer. She
already knew how to do that. No, this was more
about shifting her mindset to possibility and making
something happen.

I don't like to gender generalize, but I do think
that women are not taught to negotiate from a
position of strength or value. It may be that men
overestimate their value and women tend to
underestimate theirs. However, maybe all humans

could do a better job of understanding our value and getting the other person to articulate our value in the marketplace. This was something that Sherry needed to work on that would lead to greater results for her, professionally and personally.

Also, I learned early in the process that Sherry consistently received comments about how good she looked. In fact, she was aware and always made sure that she looked her best. While making a good presentation on the outside is important, (people do judge you on appearance), it pales in comparison to how you feel on the inside. That is the heart of the matter for many people. The presence you bring forth from the inside can affect how you look on the outside and definitely impacts your results. Whether it's sales, leadership, executive presence, or relationship, that is what makes a difference.

At this point, allow me to say a few words about a "time-tested" cliché: "Fake it until you make it." For years, people have been doing this. Has it worked? Of course, it has— for a few people. That's why you keep hearing the phrase. However, the vast majority of people who try this philosophy fail miserably. Is there anyone left on the planet who doesn't see through this tired, old, annoying tactic? I prefer that you tell the truth to yourself and begin to go to work on what will build your self-worth. I'll give you a hint: It's not working on your weaknesses. It's finding your strength and making it stronger. So, find your strength and do the work to build it up.

Underneath Sherry's beautiful exterior beat the heart of a lion—a champion. Sherry has the perseverance and determination to hang in there, no matter what, when it comes to selling. However, in the arena of negotiating for her own good (whether it was her compensation package or her time), she folded and acquiesced. The real key to Sherry's increased performance and the attainment of "balance" in her life was her ability to strengthen her resolve. She needed to be clear about what she wanted and what her highest priorities were.

During the time I worked with her, Sherry also began a rigorous exercise program, so she was building her outer muscles and inner muscles at the same time. The metaphor worked for her. She identified and developed an ideal week for herself and strengthened her ability to say *no* to things.

Saying *no* is a problem for a lot of people— especially women. In trying to be nice and be liked, you find yourself trying to please people. When someone asks you to do something, you say *yes* without thinking whether or not it really serves you or is appropriate. When you say *yes* enough times, you find that your plate is full. You are overloaded and stressed. I'm not saying you need to become nasty or mean. You simply have to learn to think and, when it's appropriate, say *no*. When you prioritize your life, you can say *no* to what doesn't fit. The

better you are at saying *no*, the easier it is to
say *yes* to what works. By strengthening those
muscles, you can design the life you want
more easily.

After Sherry learned to prioritize what was most
important to her, designed her ideal week, and
found new strength in being able to say *no* to what
doesn't work, she stopped spending time on things
she didn't want to do.

Sherry renegotiated her compensation agreement,
and her sales volume increased as well. In short,
Sherry hit all the goals she set out to hit. What she
really found and took hold of, however, was herself,
a new resolve, and her family.

So, how about you? What do you need to say *no*
to? Where are you not standing up for yourself
when it counts the most? Are you living your ideal
life? Are you doing what you want to do when you
want to do it?

3

WHAT COULD A TWENTY-EIGHT-YEAR-OLD GUY POSSIBLY TELL YOU THAT WOULD MAKE A DIFFERENCE?

J ack is a brilliant thinker and creative genius out of Carnegie Mellon University. (As an interesting side note, I've noticed that within five minutes of meeting them, most graduates of Carnegie Mellon and Harvard let you know that they graduated from there. There are exceptions to this, but Jack wasn't one of them. Still, I found him to be bright, intriguing, and a good person.)

We met at a networking event through a center of influence and advocate of mine, Ann Dugan. Jack had been enrolled in one of her programs at the Institute for Entrepreneurial Excellence at the Katz Graduate School of Business at the University of Pittsburgh; she thought there would be synergy between Jack and me, and she was right (as usual).

When we met, Jack was the president of an advertising and branding firm. This was highly unusual for such a young man. He hired me to improve his presentation skills when he was in front of the room. He felt good when addressing his staff, but uncomfortable in front of strangers. He envisioned more presentations in his future and wanted to be better.

In return, Jack helped me with my branding and got me clearer about who my main markets were and how best to reach them. He also wanted my materials to be more consistent and uniform in message and look.

Jack was starting a new venture: a whole new
business and direction. He was an expert at
developing websites and brands for businesses, and
he was looking to focus on physicians and medical
practices. The biggest problem turned out to be
that most of his prospects were baby boomers, and
he was Generation X. Also, there was a disconnect
between his service and his message.

It was easy for him to assume that in terms of
marketing, his prospects weren't smart enough
to understand what he was talking about. Many
factors contributed to this conclusion. Doctors
aren't thought of as good businesspeople. They
generally don't seem to know about marketing,
and they don't pay much attention to it. They
just don't understand. And last but not least,
Jack was from Carnegie Mellon, after all.

There is a concept called "Smartest Person
in the Room Syndrome." You probably
know people who have to impress you as

being smarter than anyone else. It can be really annoying to everyone around them. Sometimes, it can be intimidating, especially when the person is the boss or team leader. It gets in the way of communication and, over time, it is always off-putting.

Jack's sales were slow and minimal, even though the concept and the product/service were revolutionary and top-notch. What could be wrong, and how could he break through?

I'm a big believer in the phrase, "It's not just what you say, it's how you say it." However, it's also how it lands. In other words, even more important than what you say and how you say it is how the other person (or audience) hears or understands it. In addition, communication also involves *who* and *how you are being* in the matter. Your demeanor can affect communication in a big way. That is one of the main things I learned from Fernando Flores. And that was the key to Jack's issue with his prospects.

Jack was twenty-eight years old dealing with physicians who were mostly in their fifties and sixties. What, do you imagine, was the monologue going on in his prospects' minds? Most baby boomers (especially professional people) are not open to listening to what a person in his or her twenties has to say about anything. Most are of the opinion that younger folks think they know everything about everything when, in reality, they don't know squat.

Therefore, they may become more than bored or disinterested in the conversation. They may become angry and agitated. And when the younger person actually *does* know what he or she is talking about, older people can actually become even *more* upset. They may start to think about all of the things that they don't know and how time may have passed them by.

All of that was what Jack was "speaking" into when he attempted to "sell" his idea and service.

One more thing: When you are at your best, you aren't selling anything. You are enrolling someone into the possibility that your product, service, or idea could be for them.

> No one wants a website. No one wants your product or service, either. So, stop selling your product or service. You heard me: Stop *selling* your product or service. What people want is some result. Hopefully, your product or service will help them get it. That's the key. Find out what they want and see if your offering fits.

That is the mindset that ultimately transformed Jack's results. He no longer attempted to convince people about his service; now, he found out what they wanted and helped them figure out how his idea would help them get it.

Then we worked on Jack's opening statement, which spoke to the conversation that was already going on inside the prospects' heads. We had him address the basic issue some baby boomers have with a young buck. We redesigned his opening with the following:

Doctor, right now you are probably asking yourself, "What could a twenty-eight-year-old guy possibly have to say that could make a difference to me or my practice?" (Pause) I understand your thinking. A lot of my peers are full of crap, but we think that we know everything there is to know. (Pause) However, I think I have something that could actually revolutionize your practice and simplify your life. Would you be open to having a conversation about that?

With no other change in his presentation, Jack's sales increased 67 percent. When he added the other steps of the Goldman Enrollment Process (see Appendix A), sales ultimately exceeded 300 percent, and his new company skyrocketed.

While the revised opening represented something new for Jack to say, the real shift occurred in how he was *being*. Jack learned to acknowledge who he was in the conversation in relation to his audience. It didn't matter whether he was one-to-one or one-to-many; Jack became responsible for himself and the listener, and his communication improved — especially his listening. He also became a more effective speaker. Today, his company is thriving, and his customers are thrilled.

So, how about you? Are you too busy "selling" and not finding out what your customer really wants? Are you trying to convince your audience instead of listening to them? Do you even know who your perfect audience/customer is?

4

SERIOUSLY, WHY AM I COACHING *YOU?*

I understand where Bob was coming from. I experienced the same feelings six years prior to when I met him.

He was healthy. His wife and seven children were all healthy. He possessed everything that should make someone happy (most people only wish they could have what Bob had). He had a 12,000-square-foot house with an indoor swimming pool in a beautiful section of town, two great cars, a successful business that paid deep six figures, a net worth of over $10 million, a few side businesses to keep him interested, and a couple hobbies that he was good at doing—speaking, writing, and golf. It was The American Dream.

Bob reached out to me and hired me to increase his income and net worth and be able to spend more time with his family. We became friends as well because early in our relationship, Bob realized that I was not chasing his fame and fortune. Apparently, there is no shortage of people who are willing to use him and "grab" his money. When you work with people who are already successful, that is a fear and a hurdle you must overcome. During the coaching process, we discovered some additional issues.

Bob was brought up in a successful family business and was motivated by the carrot-and-the-stick method. It is a very effective method for training donkeys and other animals to pull heavy loads. In this technique, the carrot is placed in an animal's view so the animal continues to move toward it (yet it never catches it). The stick is used to keep the animal's focus on the carrot. This was also widely used to establish the American Industrial Revolution mindset.

Bob's father was a big believer in it; Bob was raised in that mindset. The carrot/stick method produces results in the short run, and can still be seen in programs like sales quotas, market share analyses, and various leadership initiatives.

The problem with it is the residual effect. One feels that no matter how much you produce or how far you progress, it's never enough. *You still need more.*

This was Bob's real issue. No matter how much he achieved, earned, possessed, or sought after, he was never happy. Let that sink in for a moment. Bob already had what most of you are striving for, and he still wasn't happy.

Allow me to say a few words about the Comparison Trap. Do not compare yourself to others. You may use other people's examples to help motivate you. However, when you compare yourself to someone else, you lose in two ways. First, you almost never compare yourself down. Most of the time, you compare yourself to someone that you think is doing better than you are. Even when you are doing as well as Bob, you compare yourself to those who do even better. And he did that.

Secondly, you compare your insides to their outsides. In other words, you are comparing how you feel to how they look...and, it's your perception of how they look. You cannot win that game. So don't play it.

Don't get me wrong here, it's not a bad thing to want more. There's nothing wrong with pursuing your dreams—wanting more— going for the gusto. The key is to be happy with what you have while you pursue what you want.

That is where the coaching process turned, and now Bob had a new goal and direction: How to be satisfied (happy) with what you have while you pursue what you want.

To go one step further, the real key to having more (and maybe even having it all) is to be *grateful* for what you have while you pursue what you want.

There is a sales and management philosophy that says, "Never be satisfied; always be striving." Managers believe that this will keep their people motivated and producing greater results. *Only in the short run.* Over time, this philosophy produces stress, burnout, and poor performance.

You know if your organization operates according to that kind of thinking. As I said before, that carrot/stick philosophy will produce results—up to a point. And then it almost always falls short in the long run. What I found, and what Bob certainly experienced, is that being happy and grateful with what you have while you pursue what you want is much more satisfying.

When Bob discovered what the real issue was, he really kicked it into gear. With his newfound appreciation for everything he already possessed, he relaxed and began producing unprecedented results. Bob was already an achiever; he didn't need me for that. But now he became a happy, contented man. Gratitude became his mindset, and achievement was no longer a struggle. His business grew, his personal life flourished, and his whole world expanded.

Today, Bob is retired from his business (although he still occasionally consults and speaks). He is still happily married. His children are all married. In addition, he has twenty-three grandchildren. His net worth has more than doubled, and he is living a truly great life. Not because he has achieved so much more; because he learned to appreciate what he already had while pursuing whatever is next.

So, how about you? Are you grateful for what you have? "But wait," you might say, "I don't have what I want yet." You can still be grateful for what you do have while you pursue what you want. Think: What are you grateful for right now? I'll give

you the first one. *You're alive.* Here's another—
you're able to read and understand this book. Come
up with a few more things and keep them in mind
while you go after your dream.[3]

---

[3] For more on gratitude see Appendix B: G.O.L.D. Attitudes.

5

DO YOU WANT TO WIN THE BATTLE OR TRIUMPH IN THE END?

Louise was unique—one of a kind. She was the only woman in the United States selling her specialty steel product. I was hired to help with her "behavioral problem" and increase her sales volume. At our first meeting, Louise outlined what she wanted to achieve from our coaching relationship.

Certainly, she wanted to increase her sales, have more fun in her life (perhaps find the love of her life), be a better manager, and get all the men

around her to respect her for who she was. I sensed
an immediate connection between what she saw
as disrespect and what management saw as a
behavior problem.

During our first few sessions, Louise let me know
what it was like in the marketplace, and in her own
office, to be the only woman selling her product.
Brutal doesn't quite cover how bad the attitude of
men was toward her. To say the least, it wasn't easy
to make a living, and the pressure from the vice
president of sales increased daily. In fact, sometimes
that battle was tougher than making sales calls to
factories. Louise found herself in a constant battle
for respect, understanding, and results.

There seemed to be conflict all around her. I had
to watch myself to make sure that I didn't become
part of the problem. After all, as a male, it would be
easy to lump me into the mix as well.

Upper management in Louise's company (all
male) found her to be abrasive. Other salespeople

with whom she worked around the country (all
male) found her to be bossy. Customers (all
male) found her to be pushy. I understood her
frustration because she saw herself as a good-
hearted person who just wanted to be respected
and produce results.

We worked on the concept of *beingness* and the
distinction between how we perceive ourselves
and how others see us. This is literally a study of
how and whom you are being, at any moment.
Stephen Covey, in *7 Habits of Highly Effective
People*, called this seeing through lenses. He said
that often the way we "see" the problem is the
problem. In fact, the problem could be the "lens"
you are using to see what you think is the problem.
Louise understood the distinction, but had some
difficulty with the concept that the vast majority of
knowledge and information falls into the category
of *you don't know what you don't know.*

You *know* what you know, and you *know* what you don't know. In other words, there is plenty that you don't know, and you *know* that you don't know it. However, most of the really valuable insight into human behavior and response falls into the category of things you don't know, and you also *don't know* that you *don't know them.*

In addition, while most human beings like to be right about things, some of us have a stronger need than others to be right. Louise suffered from this. Even worse, she happened to be right about this issue. That made it easier for her to dig in her heels and become more and more righteous. That made her situation tougher.

She finally broke through and understood completely when I compared her situation to Joan of Arc. Louise had a choice in the matter. She could continue to be Joan of Arc, the female representation of how women ought to be treated at work and in the marketplace, continually fighting the "good fight" and standing up for what's right, pitting herself against her opponents—colleagues and prospects. Or she could use her power and influence as a woman (the only woman in her industry, remember) to her advantage, stop fighting, and achieve the results she wanted.

I'm not suggesting that you accept it when something goes against your principles or values. Fighting is rarely the way to get what you want. Find a better way to achieve a result. Listening for understanding is generally better than arguing, screaming, or pouting. Remember, as Covey said, the key to getting someone to listen to you is to listen to them first.

I was careful not to suggest which option was right or wrong; only that she had a choice, and each choice had consequences. (They always do.) I always talk with my clients about staying away from the arena of Right vs. Wrong and playing instead in the arena of Most Effective Response to the Circumstance. As humans, we have a choice of response to what happens. You always have a choice, and the choice will have consequences or outcomes.

You have no choice over a knee-jerk reaction. When you go to the doctor and have your reflexes tested with a little hammer, your knee jerks. So it is with your reactions to circumstances. There is always an initial reflexive response. Rarely is it the most effective response. Yet, you know people who go around having one knee-jerk response after another. Question: Is that the way you want to live? Can you think of a better response?

Louise could have chosen to be Joan of Arc. I reminded her that things didn't turn out so well for Joan. She was burned at the stake. Her life ended poorly. She did, however, achieve sainthood, and

500 years later, we are still talking about her. So, if Louise chose to continue to fight the fight, she might also be remembered as a leader for women's rights in the workplace. Certainly, she would continue to enhance her reputation as a rebel.

Conversely, Louise could choose to use her wiles, intelligence, and feminine outlook to her advantage and achieve astounding results.

> Women and men have a different way of focusing in life. Men, for the most part, focus like a laser beam and work on one thing at a time. Women have a more holistic way of looking at things and see the whole picture in a better way. Both ways of focus are important and valuable. We all can learn so much from one another. One is not necessarily better than the other.

> I believe that in general, women are smarter than men in a lot of ways. In terms of sales and leadership, they are far superior because

they listen better than men. However, I also
believe that if they are really smart, especially
in sales and leadership, women will allow men
to think that they are smarter.

So in Louise's situation, her choice became one
of who she wanted to be in life: Joan of Arc, the
fighter, who goes toe-to-toe with the other person?
Or the kind, good-hearted person who wanted
respect and results? She realized that all she needed
to do was to be the person she is and allow that to
come through and give up the constant battle.

When she did so, sales increased, other
salespeople began requesting that she accompany
them, and her management/leadership star began
to rise as she gained the respect she wanted.
What she really gained was the insight that she
could just be herself and didn't have to fight for
everything—a triumph indeed.

On a personal note, when she chose to give up the fight, her personal life got better as well. She ended up married to one of the executives she had previously fought with so much.

So, how about you? Are you fighting for attention, recognition, or results? Are you demanding things be a certain way? Are you seen or known as a rebel or troublemaker? How can you be more relaxed, in the moment, and still achieve results without fighting all the time? Could the problem you think you have be the way you are *looking* at it?

6

I'M VERY SKEPTICAL ABOUT THIS; WILL IT STILL WORK?

I've coached a few people over the years who were highly skeptical of the process. They questioned whether or not coaching would actually produce a result. Two clients come to mind when I think about this. Although they hired me for different reasons, they were similar in attitude and reached the same breakthrough in their lives.

George is a financial advisor who produced well but knew he could be doing a lot better. His skeptical, sardonic attitude served him well when managing risk in his life. He was quick-witted, smart, and very sarcastic. As a result, his clients loved him and

as he reported, always looked forward to meeting
with him. He wanted to increase his production
and revenue, get more referral business, and have
more time for fun in his life. I assured him that he
could produce those results even if he came into the
program as a skeptic.

George had a particular view of motivational
speakers, and I assured him that this was a lot
more than just motivation. Besides, all motivation
is self-motivation. If I'm lucky, perhaps I can
create a spark which ignites something inside that
motivates you to produce a result. Clearly, the
motivation comes from inside. The key is doing
the work. You can do it with a smile, or you can
do it kicking and screaming along the way. As
long as you engage and do the work, you will
produce the result.

What won George over was something one of my
mentors said. Jim Rohn was famous for saying that
a lot of people thought that what he did was just
motivation; all you have to do is motivate someone.

But, he said, "If you have an idiot, and you motivate him, now you have a motivated idiot." That's not good. If someone is going down the wrong path in life, you don't want to accelerate *that* process.

We began to explore the procedures that George used to run his business. What markets did he pursue? How did he reach them? What did he say when he met someone? We discussed his goals for his business. What were his monthly, weekly, and daily action plans for achieving his targets? Then we designed a plan and an organization for how he would operate his ideal business model inside of his ideal life. We set benchmarks which would keep him accountable for results. While being accountable to someone else (like a coach) can be helpful, it is essential to be accountable to yourself. All of this was extremely helpful to George because it provided a structure for his business that had been previously lacking.

The real breakthrough occurred when we looked at how he communicated to the marketplace, his family and friends, and to himself. We explored his style, and I finally asked the essential question. Is being sarcastic, defensive, and protective the way you want to go through life? Is it OK? Does it really serve you well? After all, at the very least, it takes a lot of energy to be that way. I mean, it's exhausting.

> I know a little bit about this because for thirty years (age fifteen to forty-five) that's how I operated in life. Always quick with a comment. Sarcastic. Thinking I was clever or funny. What I realized was that it was a huge defense mechanism to protect myself. What I didn't want anyone to know or find out is that I wasn't good enough. In short, I didn't like myself and I compensated by being a smart-ass. It's exhausting.

George admitted that he was tired most of the time and found it to be a lot of pressure to come up with witty things to say all the time. It was as if he was always "on" —performing for an audience constantly. I suggested that it didn't have to be that way; there were alternative ways of being.

I asked, "What if you were vulnerable enough to just be yourself?" Keep in mind that George was successful. So, his being sarcastic and defensive was working for him. I wondered, "What if being more authentic could produce an even better result?" Was there business he was *not* getting because of how he was being? Was change at least worth a try?

The real turnaround was that George took control or ownership of his sarcasm. Before the coaching program, sarcasm owned George. In other words, he couldn't *not* be sarcastic. There was no choice. You said something and George came back with a witty quip.

Now, George owned it and controlled it. He could choose to be sarcastic when he wanted to, or he could choose not to. He was the driver. It didn't happen overnight; it took practice and discipline to achieve these results.

After one year, George's business had more than doubled. It continues to grow years later. More importantly, his relationships with his family, friends, clients, and colleagues improved, and George is a happier human being.

So, how about you? Are you being a certain way to protect yourself from others "finding out" about you? Are you skeptical about everything? If you allowed yourself to be more vulnerable, could your results be even better? More importantly, could you possibly be happier?

7

THERE WAS TROUBLE
IN PARADISE

Although he performed a different service and hired me for different results, Steve was almost exactly like George. Steve was CEO of a public company, and his board suggested that coaching might improve his behavior and results with his team and staff. A few coaches were interviewed for the assignment, and I was one of two finalists for the project.

Then the company decided to fire Steve instead of hiring a coach.

That made the other coach the right choice at the time because she had HR experience with outplacement. Steve intimated, however, that he thought we were a good fit, and he had never forgotten something I had told him; if he could get to a place where he replaced frustration with fascination, he could control his sarcasm and skepticism. In other words, he could own being skeptical and sarcastic and *choose* when to use it; it wouldn't be an automatic response.

About a year later, I got a call from Steve. He had started a consulting practice and wanted to hire me to grow the business. There were a few other incidental items, but the main thrust of the program was to increase revenue.

We began right away, and results came quickly. The fact is that Steve was and is really good in his field: a certified expert who sees things that others can't. We talked about how to structure deals, how to word the proposal, how to charge for value and not just for time. I had him read *Million Dollar Consulting* by Alan Weiss—the Bible for consultants.[4]

---

[4] Weiss, Alan. *Million Dollar Consulting*. New York, (NY: McGraw–Hill Education, 1992, 2016.)

Alan is still one of the gurus I turn to and
recommend for others.

Steve did all the work and made incredible progress.
In very little time, he had accomplished the goal of
making the income he had made when I first met
him, and he was his own boss. Steve was thriving.

> At this point, allow me to say something
> about being your own boss or being the boss.
> Some people embark on this journey because
> they don't want to deal with other people
> or bureaucracy. They want to get away from
> politics and others' agendas. However, please
> remember this: You still have to answer to
> someone. It may be a board of directors, or it
> may be the clients you work with. You are still
> responsible to somebody.

There was still something under the surface that
was bothering Steve and me. While he was doing
very well, something was not quite right, and we
couldn't put our finger on it. I had an inkling that

it had something to do with his sarcasm. Maybe it was insecurity or some deep-seated factor. I'm not a psychologist. And then, he threw me a curve.

He came into a session with a dilemma. He had been offered a CEO position with one of his clients. It would mean that he would have to suspend or give up his consulting practice. But they were offering a lot of money and perks, and he could move back to the east coast. Moreover, Steve determined that the CEO position might be the solution to that something inside that wasn't being satisfied.

I wasn't so sure.

He took the job.

He was excited; I should have been. The new position automatically fulfilled the increased revenue goals of our agreement. Still, I wasn't sure. Steve moved to the east coast, and we talked a few times over the next few months. But for all intents and purposes, our agreement was now complete.

Then, around six months later, I received a call from Steve. There was trouble in paradise. It seems the deal wasn't as good as it had initially sounded, and the new position wasn't working out. Worse yet, the blame was falling on Steve—the definition of *Horrible Fit*.

> My coach, Mark LeBlanc, has a definitive explanation of *Right Fit* and *Wrong Fit*. There are three categories of *Right Fit* and three categories of *Wrong Fit*:[5]
>
> Perfect Fit
> Right Fit
> Good Fit
> _____
> Bad Fit
> Wrong Fit
> Horrible Fit

---

[5] LeBlanc, Mark and Henry DeVries. *Build Your Consulting Practice.* Oceanside, CA: Indie Books International, 2017.

When you are enrolling clients or customers, you really want to concentrate on *Right Fit* and *Perfect Fit*. Maybe there are twenty to twenty-five characteristics that make up what would be a perfect fit for you and your operation. Whether you are in your own business, working for someone else, looking for the perfect job, or even assessing someone you want to be in a relationship with on a personal level, you want to determine what are the twenty to twenty-five characteristics of a perfect fit for you.

By contrast, when enough characteristics are missing, you move down the scale until it could become a wrong fit. The definition of *Horrible Fit* is when it is a wrong fit *and* they make it *your fault*.

That's where Steve was, and now he was calling me for my advice.

We discussed his options moving forward. At least the company was willing to give him a severance package as part of his leaving. We agreed on three more sessions to get clear about Steve's next move. In those sessions Steve became clear about what had been getting in the way of his satisfaction and relationships for his entire life.

The roots of his sarcasm, his skepticism, and his wanting the security of a job were feelings of unworthiness. It was all wrapped up in his feeling that he wasn't good enough.

Once he discovered that he was as good at his job as people thought, he could proceed in his own consulting practice. He put himself back out in the marketplace as an expert in the field, and his first client became the company where he had just been CEO. They realized that Steve was not the problem after all, and they really needed his expertise. Buoyed by that, he landed more engagements, and Steve has never looked back again. He is living the life he has always dreamed of as his own boss, calling his own shots. Steve had hired me to solidify and increase his business (which he did), and, along the way, he found himself—a worthy, good man.

So, how about you? Where are you feeling unworthy, that if you could shift how you see yourself, you could become your best self? You may have to work on becoming an expert, or you may just have to discover where you are already an expert. It helps to listen to the marketplace. People will let you know what they think you are good at. Listen to them. In addition, determine the characteristics of who would be a *Perfect Fit*.

8

HER SELF-TALK UNDERMINED HER AT EVERY TURN

Michelle had trouble pulling the trigger. She wanted the results of increasing her business, making more money, having more time for herself (balance), and achieving a level of recognition in her company. Most, if not all, of her coworkers were men. Her boss treated her like an administrative assistant/confidant even though she was in sales. She noted that she didn't feel respected for her production or expertise. She wanted to be the number one salesperson, and in her own words, "kick their asses."

She just wasn't sure that my coaching program could produce the results she wanted. I assured her that it wouldn't. The *program* doesn't produce the result; she does. The key distinction in any program or process is that the person produces the results. In fact, that's part of the agreement that my clients sign. They need to be clear that they are responsible for producing the result. The program is a catalyst— a tool to help make results happen. The coach holds them accountable for doing what must be done.

Not only did Michelle need to trust the program and me, Michelle needed to trust herself. I also assured her that if she did the work, she would produce the results, and that I would not let her down. Finally, she hired me.

What we discovered in the first few sessions was that Michelle had an issue with trust, commitment, focus, and clear direction. When she made a decision or choice, she would automatically consider all the other alternatives. She knew her markets and her product. She knew what she could do for people and why her product worked for them. The issue was one of clarity and certainty in communicating it. Being able to articulate your offering makes it easier for people to buy. When you're not sure, they are not sure.

I found out finally what was underneath the issues for Michelle. Like Joe, in the first story, Michelle had a belief system that was tarnished by her upbringing and the fact that she had never gone to college.

Allow me to assert, once more, that while going to college from age eighteen to twenty-two is an amazing experience, it is not necessary for success in life. One can always go later and pick up a degree if that's important. One can never get the experience of being eighteen to twenty-two again.

However, you can be very successful (especially in sales) without a degree, or even having attended college. Unless...you don't believe that. If you think you are somehow inferior, less than, not as good as, or cannot express yourself well because you didn't go to college, that belief will affect your results in every area of life.

When Michelle opened up to me and told me her story, I saw how she had created a series of beliefs that held her back from achieving the results she really wanted. More importantly, she began to see how her self-talk and belief system caused her lack of results.

Michelle had a lot going for her. As I mentioned, she knew her product, her industry, her client base, and how to sell. On top of that, she is very attractive and has a warm, charming, and friendly personality. However, her self-talk undermined her at every turn. There was where we needed to do the work.

Self-acceptance is a tricky thing. How do you learn to accept yourself for who you are (warts and all) and maybe even like yourself just as you are? So many of us fall into the trap: "I'll be happy when___ ," as if there is something missing, and that if you could just fill in the blank, then you would be happy. Or maybe you think it's outside of you: "If I had the right house, or spouse, or car, or job, or salary, or net worth," or whatever. How do you become comfortable in your own skin?

We developed a marketing strategy and an action plan that was easy to follow, and Michelle seemed to like the simple routine of knowing what to do and doing it. She started setting up and closing more business. Selling more and making more deals does wonders for your self-esteem; you are actually producing results.

However, for self-acceptance, you have to go deeper. You have to change your self-talk. You have to make friends with that voice in your head that constantly criticizes you. And you can do it.

When you notice that you are being critical of yourself, you can choose to smile and acknowledge it. *There is that little voice again.* You don't have to believe it. It's a choice you make.

You might say, "Oh no…it's the truth! I'm not a very good person." And then follow up with a list of evidence you can use to prove it.

Nonsense. That response is a choice. You can choose another response—another interpretation.

You have the opportunity to start being a good person right now, no matter what you have done in the past.

Michelle believed that she wasn't smart enough to succeed. She wasn't good enough to talk to and serve successful people. She believed that because she never went to college, she wasn't worthy of success.

However, as she started to do the work, she sold more business and produced results. She started to see that her beliefs were getting in her way and they were just not true. Michelle was smart, beautiful, warm, friendly, capable, and ultimately, successful.

She hired me to produce results and become the best salesperson in her office. What she really got from the engagement was self-worth and dignity. She is now OK with herself just the way she is and has even grown to like who she is. She tells me that she still has her moments, but they are fewer, and she snaps out of them more quickly. You can, too.

Oh, and by the way: She ended up being the number one producer and kicked the guys' asses in the process.

So, how about you? What are you telling yourself that gets in the way of producing results? What are you waiting for to appear in your life before you can be happy? Where are you selling yourself short?

9

YOU ARE RESPONSIBLE (RESPONSE-ABLE)

I received a call from a company with which I had done business years ago. They had a behavior problem with a senior executive who was bullying his direct reports. Since Peter was a shareholder, a project manager, and the leader of a group of project managers, they didn't want to fire him. In addition, he was one of the top rainmakers in the firm. In short, he was valuable. Perhaps I could coach him to behave better and be a model employee. This is not my normal type of assignment, and I wasn't sure if it would be a good fit. However, I agreed to meet Peter to see.

A large, bald, imposing figure (reminiscent of Mr. Clean) entered the room on the appointed day. Peter is six foot four and 250 pounds, with a very serious demeanor. We chatted for an hour or so about what he would want to get from a coaching program and why we would even embark on such a journey. He was certainly aware of why I was there, but ultimately disagreed with the premise that he was the problem.

I have since learned that this is a very common theme among bully employees. "It's not my fault; people aren't producing or doing their jobs!"

The reason I accepted the challenge was that I liked Peter. There was an authenticity about him, and in addition, he truly wanted to be a better person and produce greater results. It was an opportunity for me to make a real difference in someone's life, and he was eager to get started.

We met every week for the first few months of a year-long agreement. Peter would outline the way the organization operated and how frustrating it was to get things accomplished. He continued to deflect the cause of the problem to others around him. Without disagreeing with him, I had to help him shift the focus and responsibility back to himself. Not because it was his *fault*; because that's ultimately where the power to change things resides.

> The only way you can have any power or control of a situation is if you take responsibility for it. You cannot change someone else's behavior; you can only change yourself. The place to concentrate is on your response to circumstances. You cannot change what happened; you can choose and change your response to it. As Jim Rohn used to say, "If you change (your response), everything will change for you." He also said (one of my all-time favorites), "The winds of circumstance blow on us all. The set of your sail determines your outcome."

Until Peter saw that his responses and behavior affected how others behaved around him, no progress would be made. We spent a long time on this one. It's not about who is right and who is wrong; it's about being *able* to choose the most effective (or at least a more effective) response to circumstances.

The first habit in Stephen Covey's *7 Habits of Highly Effective People* is "Be Proactive."[6] Most people define this as taking action. However, it's more than that. In fact, if you go back and read that chapter, you will see that Covey italicized the word *responsible* when he said that being proactive is when you are *responsible* for the actions you take.

He then defined *responsible* as if it were two words: Response–Able—literally, the ability to respond more effectively to a circumstance. *Brilliant!*

---

[6] Stephen R. Covey, *The 7 Habits of Highly Effective People* (Provo, UT: Franklin Covey, 1998).

Until you are able to take responsibility for your
life, you will continue to be at the mercy of
circumstances. Until Peter could be responsible for
his behavior, nothing would progress—even if he
were right.

One new behavior that worked was getting Peter
to smile more often. Instead of being serious and
intense all of the time, a simple smile could change
others' interpretation of his message.

Peter finally got it. He saw that his response to
circumstances affected outcomes. In fact, he could
influence and control situations with his response.
He now had a new game to play: Become a more
effective leader, project manager, and business
development person by responding more effectively
and taking ownership of his behavior. His results
began to skyrocket.

As Peter became more adept at this process,
another issue became more apparent. The
organization did not support his progress. It seemed

as if they were looking for a scapegoat to blame
for others' ineffectiveness. In fact, the behavior
that Peter was accused of was the very behavior
exhibited by his boss. Could that possibly be what
was happening? This would shift the momentum of
the assignment. Thus began a new game: How do
you play win/win when the other side is committed
to playing win/lose?

> When you are in a selling situation or some
> negotiation where it becomes obvious that the
> other person is playing win/lose, then you can
> adopt the philosophy of win/win or no deal.
> Simply stated, if we cannot agree on a way to
> both win, let's just not play, for now.

However, when the person running the game is
your boss or your spouse, it becomes a bit more
challenging. Of course, you can still walk away, but
there are consequences. Peter was not ready to
walk away from his job, so he had to figure out a
way to deal with a bully who called him a bully. It

would take communication skills, and in particular, listening in a different way.

You must remain curious, which causes you to inquire and ask for greater understanding without causing the other person to become defensive. With a lot of practice, Peter became adept at navigating the choppy waters of doubt, scrutiny, and accusation. He began producing greater results, and more importantly, became more comfortable in his own skin, despite the swirl of chaos around him.

In time, he finally realized that he was in the wrong organization and moved on, but not before he learned some valuable lessons about communication, people, and leadership in general.

So, how about you? Where are you pointing fingers of blame and relinquishing responsibility for yourself and your behavior? Can you see things from a different perspective? Are you aware of another point of view? Practice owning your part of the situation and exercise the muscle of choosing a more effective response.

10

CONCLUSION

The journey toward happiness has been a long, arduous one. When it began, I'm not even sure that I knew it was a journey. At first, it seemed that it was about being accepted by others. Perhaps it was about success, accomplishment, and doing well. You know: get good grades, be liked, get into the "right" club or group, go to the "right" college, find the "right" mate, a good job, etc., etc., etc. All of that was what would make you happy.

John Lennon was right back in fourth grade. He knew what he wanted in life. He knew the secret —*be happy*. But what was going to make that happen? Ultimately, you find out that the journey is about self-acceptance and self-love.

This has been my journey for my entire life: the search for self-esteem, self-acceptance, and self-love.

All of those things you chase early on are not the answer. They are necessary steps along the way. After each accomplishment, however, you are still left with the question, "Is that all there is?" So, you keep searching.

So how about you? Where are you on the scale of self-acceptance? Do you constantly beat yourself up, or do you accept and like yourself, warts and all?

Also, along the way, there are milestone moments—key events that perhaps you are aware of, perhaps not. These milestones end up defining the journey, and they define you.

In each of the foregoing stories, the protagonist set out to attain something, and along the way, found something greater—themselves. In most cases, they also achieved the desired results. But the much greater reward was that of self-acceptance and happiness. That ensured ongoing results.

I have been fortunate to be the catalyst for these breakthroughs. I enjoyed the opportunity to guide them along their paths. I have also mentioned a few key milestones in my own journey. In 1978, I participated in est Training—the beginning of what is now Landmark Education; indeed, a significant milestone. Working with Fernando Flores in 1983–84 was amazing. In 1988–89, the real turning point occurred in my life.

In the summer of 1988, Duke Burns, an insurance client of mine, invited me to go to a seminar led by Brian Tracy. Brian said many insightful things that afternoon. Not anything new that I hadn't heard before, but I heard them in a way that caused me to take action for the first time in my life.

The first concept was part of his seven-step plan for success. He said that he had found the *secret* to *success*. I leaned in because I really wanted to know. Perhaps you are doing that right now.

He said that the secret to success is to have goals and write them down.

That was it.

I thought, "Yeah, yeah, yeah, I've heard that before. Tell me the *real* secret." (Just like you're doing right now.)

And then it hit me; that *was* the secret. It was something I had heard many times before, but I had never really done it. I asked myself a very important question: "What do I have to lose?"

I started the next day, and every January 1st, since 1989, I have written down my goals for the year in every category of my life that is important to me.

It works.

The second piece of Brian's advice that made an impact on me was also part of the seven-step success plan. He recommended that you read every day. Read something in your field, motivational, or inspirational every morning. It sets your tone, your mood, and your attitude for the entire day.

He said that the average person reads one book per year after they end their formal education. If you are an average reader and you read an hour per day, you will read fifty books per year. Therefore, after ten years, the average reader will have read ten books, and you will have read 500 books. Brian then asked, "Do you think that will give you an edge in the marketplace?"

One more statistic: If you study any subject for at least one hour per day, you will be an expert in three years. You could be a national expert in five years. Just one hour per day.

I asked myself, "What do I have to lose?" I started immediately, and since the summer of 1988, I have read more than 1,000 books. Do you think that would give you an edge in the marketplace? I developed an entire business around that concept. You can, too.

The third item didn't manifest until four years later, but it had a stunning impact when I heard it that day. Brian ended the seminar with the following admonition: "Life is short. Don't die with your music still inside of you."

Music has always been a big part of my life. I sang all the time, since as far back as I can remember. However, in the twenty years since I'd moved back to Pittsburgh in 1968, I had not sung. I busily built my business and raised my family, figuring that that part of my life was complete. But music is something that is in your blood. If you don't have it in yours, I can't explain it. If you do, I don't need to.

In 1992, I attended a party where there was a karaoke machine. People were taking turns getting

up to sing, and the people I was with suggested
I get up to try it. I protested and said I was done
with that part of my life, but they persisted.
Finally, I agreed and chose to sing *My Girl* by
the Temptations. Funny thing about karaoke…
when you sing *My Girl*, the backup group is the
Temptations. *WHOA*.

You couldn't get the microphone out of my hands
for the rest of the night. I realized music was
missing in my life. I was dying with my music still
inside of me.

A short time later, I was perusing the classified ads
in the newspaper. I don't know what caused me to
do that; I never read the classified ads. This blurb
popped out at me:

> BASS–BARITONE SINGER NEEDED
> FOR AN "OLDIES ROCK AND ROLL
> BAND" CALL 555-1234

I called the number. A man answered. I told him I
was calling about the ad in the paper. I said, "Are
you serious?"

He replied, "Yes. Are you serious?"

I said, "Yes and I don't mean to sound arrogant, but
I could be the answer to your prayers."

"How so?"

"Three reasons. One: While my vocal range is a
little broader, I truly am a bass/baritone. Two: I can
hear, think, and sing the harmony parts. Three: I
don't care about singing lead; I just love singing the
harmony, so I won't challenge you for lead vocals."

He told me to show up at practice on the following
Tuesday evening in a garage in Carnegie. (Carnegie
is a small suburb outside of Pittsburgh.)

There are moments in your journey when you stand at a crossroad, and you are aware that whether you turn left or right, it will have an impact on your life. What do you do?

There I was, on Tuesday evening, on my way to a garage in Carnegie. "What are you doing?" my little voice asked. "Are you crazy?" I could imagine the headlines in the morning paper: "44-Year-Old Man Found Dead in a Garage in Carnegie." But I did not turn back.

I pressed on in my quest to be the bass/baritone singer in the Magic Moments, which I have been for the past twenty-seven years. I did not die in a garage in Carnegie. I may have bombed a couple nights in a bar in Swissvale, but you get the point.

On the way to Carnegie, and in each of the stories in this book, the protagonists came to a critical moment where they faced the dragon: themselves. They started out looking for what they thought they wanted, came to the critical moment, met the challenge, and left with something far greater than what they had been looking for—they found themselves, or at least a new understanding and liking of themselves.

So how about you? What do you really want? Are you willing to face the challenges that confront you? Do you have the resolve to do whatever it takes to accomplish your goals? Will you press on and come to the glorious moment of self-acceptance? Can you find a way to actually accept and like yourself, just the way you are?

Good luck in your pursuit and enjoy the journey.

APPENDIX

A

THE GOLDMAN ENROLLMENT PROCESS

As a professional person, you really don't want to think of yourself as a salesperson. You may want to grow your business, increase your client base, and actually sell more services. However, sales is an unwelcome concept.

It's certainly a bad word. So, you refer to it as "client development" or "business development." Anything you can think of except "sales" will do. That's OK. In fact, sales is really an enrollment process.

When you are at your best, you aren't selling anything or anyone. At your best, you enroll someone into the possibility that your product or service is for them.

The Goldman Enrollment Process is a simple five-step procedure. Really, it's more than a procedure; it's a way of being. There are five steps to the process of enrolling someone into your program (selling your service).

STEP 1: *The Background Of Relationship*

First and foremost, there must be some background of relationship. Some rapport must be established. This doesn't have to be elaborate, nor does it have to take a great deal of time to do. Without it, however, nothing will go further. It could be an introduction or a referral from someone else. It could be meeting someone at a function or a business gathering. It could even be from a completely unknown source. But there must be a relationship.

You can establish this with a simple question. Ask, "What was it that made you want to meet with me today?" Then listen. That will be enough to establish that there is a relationship.

STEP 2: *The Conversation For Possibility*

This is the most important part of the process. The entire deal hinges on this piece. That might seem like a contradiction since I just mentioned that nothing happens without the background of relationship. While that's true, once there is a relationship, *possibility* is the most important part of the process.

The conversation for possibility is simply establishing the possibility that your product or service could be for the client or prospect. This is where the entire reason for your service is brought to light, in complete detail. In fact, the more said about the possibility of your offering, the better. Here's the catch: The conversation for possibility must come from the client's or prospect's mouth. So, you must ask the kinds of questions that elicit the appropriate response from the other person.

For instance, you might inquire, "What would you want to get from this process?" or "Why are you here and what do you really want?" Then, no matter what they say in response, you ask for greater understanding. And then, you say, "What else?" Keep saying, "What else?" until the other person says, "That's about it."

Remember, the entire list of things that they want must come from them—not you.

STEP 3: *The Conversation For Value*

As with the conversation for possibility, the conversation for value must also come from the prospect or client. You say, "Let's suppose that I can help you make all of the things on your list happen. What would the value of that be, in real terms, in your life?" Be prepared for them to say, "I don't know."

"I don't know" is a default answer that most people give. Here is where it comes from. When you are in elementary school, you are excited to answer questions from the teacher. Kids raise their hand and wave their arms vigorously: "Call on me! Call on me!" Until one day you raise your hand and you are called upon, and you give the wrong answer. Maybe it's a silly one. The class laughs at you. You are embarrassed and mortified. Right then and there, you make up your mind that you are never going to do that again. From that moment on, when you are called upon, you answer, "I don't know." Because the class period is 30–45 minutes long, the teacher moves on to someone else to find the answer. "I don't know" worked; it got you off the hook. Furthermore, it gets reinforced and becomes your default answer in life.

In the Enrollment Process, do not accept "I don't know." Simply say, "I realize that it's not an easy question. However, take a look. What would it be worth to you?" The person may say, "A lot." Be prepared for fuzzy, vague, general answers. You must stay focused on getting a real number that represents what the prospect thinks the value of your product or service would be. Do not browbeat or become aggressive; hang in there and get an answer. It will help you when it's time to seal the deal.

STEP 4: *The Conversation For Opportunity*

Now you get to talk about your program or service. And now you can be more focused than you have ever been. You can tailor what you have to say based on what the client is looking for. This is not meant to be manipulative in any way. If your service is not what the client is looking for, simply say so and refer someone else to the client and move on. You just saved a lot of time and trouble. However, if you are a good fit, then you can speak about your service in a very focused way. You will want to hone your talk to fifteen minutes or less.

You explain how your service works (the elements and the logistics.) Don't overdo it. Remember, less is more.

STEP 5: *The Conversation For Action*

The final step is the call to action. No matter how smoothly the rest of the process goes, you still must ask for the business. "I'm not a great salesperson. I only have one close, and I usually tell you when it's coming—pretty soon. First, do you have any questions?" Answer any questions they might have. My favorite closing question is, "On a scale of one to ten, where one means you never want to see me again and ten means you are ready to start tomorrow, where are you? What will it take to get to ten?"

You could also simply ask, "Does this make sense? Are you ready to proceed?" Or, "Here's the next step; when do you want to start?"

That's it. Simple. Effective. It works.

APPENDIX B

G.O.L.D. ATTITUDES

The winds of circumstance blow on us all; the set of your sail determines where you end up.

—JIM ROHN

A positive attitude won't get you everything in life. But, it gets you a lot more than a negative attitude does.

—ZIG ZIGLAR

The most crucial element of your life is not where you were born or when you were born. It's not where you grew up, or where you went to school, or what you do for a living, or with whom you're in a relationship. The most crucial element in your life is how you feel about all those things, and especially how you feel about yourself.

It's your attitude about all the elements of your life that makes the difference in how it turns out.

If that's true, what kinds of attitudes can lead you to a more effective, more successful and happier life? That would be an interesting discussion. I would love to hear what you think some of those attitudes would be. Meanwhile, here are four (spelling *Gold*) that can make a profound difference in how you live your life.

G: *Gratitude*

Think of five things that you are grateful for. I'll give you the first one. *You are alive.* Come up with four more.

The simple act of thinking about what you are thankful for changes everything. Gratitude can be an essential key to feeling better about yourself, and about life in general. When you focus on what's not going well, what you don't have, and what hurts, it's easy to feel bad about yourself. When you focus on the things that you're grateful for, your mood will improve instantly.

You may be grateful for many things, such as good health, all five senses functioning, the ability to think, stable relationships, love, and family. You might have different things to put in your top five. It doesn't matter what they are. The important thing is that you identify them and acknowledge them. Being aware of the good things you have shifts your perspective and totally alters the way that you go through your day.

The world is a completely abundant place. If you wake up on any given morning and think the world is an awful place, filled with horrible events and people who are out to get you, and nasty things are happening all the time, you'll find evidence wherever you look.

On the same morning, you can wake up and think the world is a beautiful place, populated with people who are out to do good things for you, and filled with wonderful and incredible experiences. Guess what? You'll find evidence all day long.

What really makes the difference in how you experience life is how you look at it. You don't have to believe me. Just try it.

When you get in touch with what you are thankful for, you begin to feel good. Another thing happens, and it's even more miraculous. When you are aware of and you acknowledge the things that make you feel grateful, you attract more abundance into your life. This is the Law of Attraction at its finest. Try it. Walk around with a genuine feeling of gratitude, and watch how many good things start happening to you.

O: *Openness*

You might think you already know what there is to know about your job, your relationships, or your life. Openness is the act of being willing to consider that there are possibilities beyond what you already know.

It's a matter of not getting caught up in your own limitations. Also, most human beings have a strong need to be right—and some have a greater need than others. Now, you're not like that, of course, but certainly, you know a lot of people who are like that, don't you? It doesn't matter if they produce results; they just have to be "right."

Part of being open is letting go of the need to be right all the time. It involves listening to other people and taking in their ideas without the notion that you've heard it all before, or you've tried that before and it didn't work, or any other kind of negative thought.

Being open requires you to step back from your preconceived notions and have the courage to ask, "What if?"

While you're reading this book, you will probably encounter concepts and practices that you've heard before. You could say to yourself, "I knew that!" It doesn't matter whether or not you knew that. The most important thing is whether or not you do it.

After all, it's not what you know; it's what you can recall in the heat of the moment and what you do that counts.

Gratitude invokes the Law of Attraction; openness invokes the Vacuum Law. This law tells you that in order to create what you want, you must remove the old before you manifest the new. You've probably experienced that feeling of freedom you get when you clean out a cluttered attic, a disorganized garage, or a messy desk. It's the rush of a new possibility—being open to what can come in, now that there is space that you did not have before. You are literally creating an opening for new things to come.

The Vacuum Law also works for the mental and emotional things that you want, such as happiness, comfort, security, and fulfillment. Just as creating a space in the physical world makes room for new things, clearing your mind and heart of negative thoughts and feelings opens you up to receiving what you desire. How do you create the vacuum, mentally or emotionally, to make room for the things you want in your life? *Forgiveness.*

The best way to open yourself to what you want in life is to forgive the things you think "happened" to you. Forgive the people you think "got one over on you," and most importantly, forgive yourself. Consider this quote, most often attributed to Gautama Buddha:

Holding a grudge is like swallowing poison and hoping that the other person is going to die.

Seriously, when you're all wrapped up in your negative feelings about someone, the other person doesn't even know (or care) about it.

You might think that if you forgive people and their acts, they are being let off the hook. In truth, when you forgive someone, you're releasing yourself— from holding on to resentments. I don't remember where I read or heard it; to "forgive" is to "give for." That means you're actually giving yourself a present, the gift of releasing the need to hold onto all of the exhausting, negative energy it takes to resent someone. In so doing, you open up space for the possibility of what could be.

In fact, true forgiving is when you say to life, "Thanks *for giving* that (situation) to me."

You will have learned something or become stronger.

Once you forgive, and you become open to possibility, amazing things can happen.

L: *Love*

John and Paul were right.

No, not the Apostles, the Beatles, when they sang "All You Need Is Love." They're not the only ones who knew how powerful love is. As you may know, the ancient Greeks had several different words for love. There was *eros*, or sexual passion; *philia*, which they said meant deep friendship; *ludus*, the kind of playful love that you might call flirting; *pragma*, the abiding love of a long-term relationship; *philautia*, the love of self; and *agape*, the love of all humankind.

The two we are going to focus on here are self-love and love of humankind, and we're going to let them work together to form a winning attitude. In much the same way as when you tap into gratitude, the world is a more welcoming and pleasant place when you truly love yourself and others.

Let's start with self-love. This doesn't mean being excessively self-absorbed, or standing around admiring yourself. Do whatever it takes to find ways to like yourself and feel secure about who you are. Seriously, take a moment to think about something you really like about yourself. It's easy to forget or take for granted your good qualities when things don't go your way.

When you get down on yourself, you tend to only see the bad, and then you pile on by allowing other bad thoughts to compound the issue. Next time (or whenever) that happens, stop and think about something you like about yourself. Like flipping a switch, you can turn a bad mood around immediately. The more you practice this, the easier it gets. You will begin to see that even when you make a mistake or life doesn't go your way, you can still love yourself. And, once you get the attitude that you are a good person, you'll be able to give the best of yourself to others.

Now let's look at the love of all humankind. When you focus on the act of being of service to others, life just gets better. That's not to say there aren't bad things that happen in the world, or that there are not some people who seem to be evil. Consider this, however: most people do the best they can, given everything they know and everything they've experienced — even the ones who seem to be evil.

I've never met anybody who has what you would call "a bad attitude." You might be thinking you have a couple of people you'd like to introduce me to, but check this out. Have you ever tried to tell

someone s/he has a bad attitude? How did that
go? If you point out someone's negative attitude,
you'll most likely get a response like, "Bad attitude?
I do not have a bad attitude! In fact, if more people
were like me, the world would be a better place!"

Life is like a movie and you are the star. Everyone is
the hero of his or her own movie. Sometimes, you
have to buy tickets to watch the movie someone
else is watching to understand how they see
themselves as the hero. Once you understand their
movie, you can understand them better. Then you
can deal with them more effectively.

You do not have to make it your mission to transform
the evil in the world. When you focus on what is
good, on what you want to have happen, on how
you want the world to be, your outlook will brighten.
This isn't just Pollyanna crap. It is a function of the
universal truth that what you think about, you bring
about. As Gandhi said, "Be the change you seek in the
world."

If you want more love, then acknowledge, give away, and focus on more love. Simply put, if you approach the world as though you truly like people, the world will be more friendly and welcoming to you.

When you're focused on a problem, that problem is all you are going to see. When you look for a solution, you begin to look past the problem. In fact, when you look past the problem, you begin to see more possible solutions.

Love helps you to become open to possibility and opportunity in your life. When you send out a loving attitude, you will find, almost miraculously, that people seem to go out of their way to do good things for you.

D: *Desire*

Desire is the one thing no one can give you. It's like a pilot light inside of you, waiting to be ignited. You have to ask yourself the question, "What do I

really want?" You may have to erase some negative
programming that tells you that it's not okay to
want things.

It's OK to want things!

Some people think it makes you a bad person to have
desires. How can you want something when there are
so many others in the world who don't have much?
I'm not suggesting to not think about other people,
but in this case, it's okay to be a little selfish.

Perhaps that inside voice about what you want
is God, Divine Presence, Higher Power, the
Universe, or whatever you call it, inspiring you
to have the things you really want. You might
not even be talking about material things. You
might want certain *attributes*, such as generosity
and confidence; maybe you want to get better
at a certain skill. The point is, when you want
something, it comes from within you, and you have
the opportunity to respond to this want and achieve
satisfaction and fulfillment.

Most of us don't let ourselves dream enough.

What do you really want, and why? Go ahead and dream.

When you identify the things you want, you then become able to summon up the courage and motivation it takes to go after them.

Light your pilot light; discover what you desire.

APPENDIX

C

ACKNOWLEDGMENTS

Most, if not all, lifetime journeys start with your childhood. Mine was good: not perfect, but relatively noneventful. So, first and foremost, I want to thank my parents and my brother for doing, as my mother would say, "The best they could." Along with many teachers in school, they provided the love and the challenges that fueled my love of learning and my search for self-acceptance.

As an adult, I have stood on the shoulders of many great teachers. I have already quoted and mentioned quite a few—Jim Rohn, Brian Tracy, Stephen Covey, Alan Weiss, Jack Canfield, and Mark

LeBlanc. Each has contributed greatly to my growth and whatever success I may have attained.

A special note about Mark LeBlanc. I have hired him twice as my coach to grow my business. In 1996, he completely shifted my mindset, which provided a quantum leap in my results. A few years ago, I hired him again, and he will be on my team forever. This book wouldn't exist without Mark. In addition, he introduced me to his partner at Indie Books International, Henry DeVries. A special thank you to Henry, his daughter Devin, Denise Montgomery, the amazing editor, and the entire team at Indie Books. They are easy to work with, and this book would not be the same without them.

A shout out to a special friend in Omaha, Nebraska. I call Kathy Larsen my "Woo-Woo Guru." Through her work, she has helped me as much as, if not more than, *anyone* in teaching me how to accept and like myself.

My children are amazing human beings. They have taught me so much about life, leadership, and love. My son Hank and my daughter Anna are my heroes and continue to inspire me. In addition, Anna typed my manuscript.

Finally, a huge *thank you* to my clients, who hired me to help them produce a result. Certainly, the nine clients whose stories are told in this book merit my gratitude. And to the hundreds of other clients, for your faith, trust, and confidence in me: thank you. It has been an incredible ride, and I appreciate you all.

APPENDIX
D

ABOUT THE AUTHOR

As founder, owner, and president of Goldman Organization, David Goldman elevates and accelerates results for professionals and executives. Since November 1989, he has worked with professionals (accountants, attorneys, and financial advisors) who want to bring in more business, and executives who want to be more effective and move up in their organizations. He consults, coaches, and teaches them to communicate more effectively so that they get the results they really want.

David also speaks to groups on various topics that get them to think, take action, and perform at a higher level.

For example, an attorney wanted to increase his revenue. When he hired David, he was billing $450,000 and collecting 50 percent of it. After one year, he was billing $950,000 and collecting 90 percent of it. Another client, a financial advisor, reported results of more than $700,000 additional new revenue over a seven-year period working with David.

As a result of his work, professionals and executives get the four Cs: more Clarity, more Certainty, more Confidence, and more Control in their communication. That leads to more revenue, more balance, better relationships, and more fulfillment.

On a personal note, since November, 1992, David has been the bass/baritone singer in the oldies rock and roll band, Magic Moments.

To reach David to purchase multiple copies of his books or to book him as a speaker, you may email him at: david@goldmanorganization.com or call him at 412-377-6200.

APPENDIX

E

WORKS CITED

Covey, Stephen R. *The 7 Habits of Highly Effective People*. Provo, UT: Franklin Covey, 1989, 1998.

Goldman, David. "Are You Listening?" Essay. In *The Sales Coach: Selling Tips from the Pros*. Monroeville, PA.: Jeffrey Tobe, 1997.

LeBlanc, Mark and Henry DeVries. *Build Your Consulting Practice*. Oceanside, CA: Indie Books International, 2017.

Weiss, Alan. *Million Dollar Consulting*. New York, NY: McGraw–Hill Education, 1992, 2016.